Copyright © 1990 by Diane Elaine Snyder

This book is dedicated to my husband, Warren,
for his encouragement, insight, and help on this project.

The FRUIT OF HER HANDS

Published by Focus on the Family Publishing, Colorado Springs, Colorado 80920.
Distributed in the U.S. and Canada by Word Books, Dallas, Texas.

Editor: Gwen Weising
Cover Fabric: S. J. Harris Company

Printed in the United States of America 93 94 95 96 97 98/10 9 8 7 6 5 4 3 2 1

Introduction

Today's Christian woman shoulders many responsibilities. As she attempts to get everything done, she often encounters frustrating circumstances that cause the important to be crowded out by the urgent.

Her most valiant efforts to consistently study God's Word, pray, and exercise repeatedly meet with distractions.

In time, discouragement sets in, and motivation to keep her goals–those set with such initial hope and zeal–fades.

The *Fruit of Her Hands Planner* is designed to take you beyond planning and into reaping the fruit of whatever goals you seek or desire to be shown in your life.

This planner helps you:
- Plan your day more efficiently
- Develop positive, godly habits
- Determine target areas that need work
- Plan practical steps to reap a harvest of organized living.

As you fill out the day-to-day activities, you will be reminded of the important goals you are trying to accomplish.

Scripture verses that are both encouraging and uplifting have been provided throughout the book. A self-check section will help you see the development of good fruit in your life.

As the Holy Spirit helps you put God's Word into practice, you will be fruitful to His glory. Your life will take on a new dimension as you learn to be a faithful caretaker of the time He has given you.

Reaping the Harvest

Here's the plan for reaping a rich harvest:

1. Determine a "seed"–a goal or positive habit–you would like to see germinate in the first week. Write it on the line under "SEED YOU WOULD LIKE TO DEVELOP THIS WEEK."

Writing down your goal will immediately cause you to focus upon it.
The seed could be an area of spiritual growth–like dealing more patiently with others. Or it could be in the area of personal development–such as exercising, budgeting, or some area of family interest.

2. PLANT your good seed by listing specific daily actions that will help you produce the fruit you desire for the week. Practice them consistently.

The hope of the harvest is in the seed, but for it to grow, it must not be neglected but watered and nurtured regularly.

3. Write down words of encouragement, inspiring thoughts, and helpful words from others in the section "WATERING THE SEED."
God's own Word will prove the greatest reservoir of strength and inspiration to you in those areas you seek to improve.

4. Under the "SELF-CHECK" section, encourage yourself by putting a code letter in a circle that relates to the current day of the week. Some ideas for codes might be "G" (for good), "T" (for trying), or use a simple check mark.

5. At each new week's beginning, evaluate your previous week's PLAN.
Remember ~ Rarely does any plan work 100 percent satisfactorily the very first time it's tried. So be patient with yourself, and you will see results.
If adjustments need to be made that will make the plan work better for you, then make them and start the next week with an adjusted PLAN.

Above all, remember, the PLANTING, WATERING, REAPING section is designed for your benefit. Therefore, do whatever is necessary to personalize it. There may be periods of time when you will not feel motivated to use this section of the planner. If so, you are in friendly company and can use any part or step that will encourage you to press on.

REAPING THE HARVEST will obviously take place over days, months, and even years and will extend into eternity! But taking a few minutes at the end of each week to reflect on the pleasant fruit you are beginning to see in your life will be richly rewarding. You will have a harvest of blessings to share with those around you.

Seed Suggestions

All of us have areas of our lives we would like to improve. Often a sermon, the words of a friend, or something we have read in God's Word will bring to light our desire to grow in certain attitudes or actions. Provided here is a list of "seeds" to start you thinking of possible areas where you might want to grow in your life. With prayer and nurturing, the harvest will reflect the fruit of these activities.

Consistent prayer life
Memorize God's Word
Regular exercise
Spiritual training of children
Watch less television
Read to my children more
Read to myself more
Be on time
Reach out to needs of others
Keep up with letter writing
Exchange worry for prayer
Establish and keep a budget
Start a hobby
Express appreciation freely
Be consistent with children
Listen and look when kids speak
Practice patience
Keep in touch with grandchildren
Be more thankful
Compliment my family
Compliment my friends
Go the extra mile
Finish half-done projects
Increase my vocabulary
Develop my gifts
Gain more job expertise
Take time to play
Extend hospitality
Value my friendships
Take care of my health
Do not put off tasks until tomorrow
Listen more to others
Encourage others more
Find more adventure in life
Keep a journal
Celebrate
Act upon God's promises
Apply the love principles of
1 Corinthians 13 to my life

Other Features of This Planner

Now that you know how to use this planner to increase good fruit in your life, here is how you can use its other features to bring more organization to each day.

MONTHLY CALENDAR AND PLANNER
- The place for planning special events, birthdays, anniversaries, and holidays.
- A handy place to keep a record of family traditions and favorite activities.
- List any preparations for special events (send birthday card, plan anniversary dinner, etc.). Then these can be transferred to the Daily Activities and Appointments section of your Weekly Calendar when you decide which day to do them.

WEEKLY CALENDAR AND PLANNER
- Dates: Write the appropriate month in the space provided on the left page. Use the line by each day to record the date.
- Daily Activities and Appointments: This section is a tracking station for what you need to do or accomplish each day. (A word to the wise–*urgent* things are often not really *important*, only urgent; and *important* things are not always *urgent*.)
- Reminders for Home and Family: This is a reminder section for providing tender loving care around the home. For example:
  Monday–change sheets
  Tuesday–start the garden with Sandy
  Wednesday–teach Charlie how to oil his baseball glove
- Personal Notes: Use as you like to plan menus, a mini-journal of special thoughts or special times with family and friends, or a spiritual journal.
- Prayer Garden: Have you ever told someone you would pray for her and then forgot to pray? Jot a note here to back up those good intentions.

SPECIAL FEATURES
- At the back of the book are six pages of instant reference to ideas and sources you need at your fingertips in categories such as books, tapes, videos, crafts, gift ideas, hospitality tips, and special menus. Have fun with these pages!

ADDRESSES AND PHONE NUMBERS
- A place for those special numbers you need to find in a hurry.

THREE–YEAR CALENDAR PAGE
- Three years at a glance.
- Special dates and holidays for each year.

See sample pages for use.

SEED YOU WOULD LIKE TO DEVELOP THIS WEEK:

Show love to those around me

PLANTING
THE
SEED

Plan daily actions that will help you produce the fruit you desire.

Patience towards my children
Look for ways to show kindness
Pray daily for God's guidance

Self-Check

S	M	T	W	T	F	S
✓	T		✓	T		✓
T	✓	✓			✓	
✓	✓	✓	✓		✓	T

T = trying

WATERING
THE
SEED

Encouragement from God's Word. Inspiring thoughts. Helpful words from others.

I. Cor. 13:4 "Charity suffereth long and is kind; Charity envieth not; Charity vaunteth not itself, is not puffed up..."

Month of:
November

DAILY
APPOINTMENTS
AND
ACTIVITIES

Sunday 13	Monday 14	Tuesday 15
9:15 Church	Write:	9:00 Bible Study
1:00 Potluck Dinner	- Thank you to Leslie	
	- Joe's B'day card	
		3:00 Drive Car Pool
6:00 Church		
Lasagne	Stir-Fry	Taco Salad

REMINDERS
FOR FAMILY
AND HOME

Day of Rest and Worship	Sew recital costumes	Read with John

PRAYER
GARDEN

Andrea - mission trip
Pam & Charles

REAPING THE HARVEST

Fruit you are seeing in your life this week as a result of God's nurturing and your faithful efforts. *(Be sure to consider little changes.)*

By trying to meet the needs of my family through patience, prayer & a few thoughtful acts of kindness, the atmosphere of our home became more peaceful. I'll work on this again next week!

"But whoso looketh into the perfect law of liberty and continueth therein, he being not a forgetful hearer, but a doer of the work, this man shall be blessed in his deed."

James 1:25

Wednesday 16	Thursday 17	Friday 18	Saturday 19
9:00 Quilt with Grandma Mitchell	11:00 To park with Grandpa and Grandma	Call: Carol & Bill Susan & Allan (To make plans for musical)	11:00 Musical— to watch Missie
Potato Soup	Hamburgers	Spaghetti	Pizza
Plan Thanksgiving Dinner	Check Sarah's schoolwork	Popcorn & Movie Night	Take kids to the library Bake cookies

PERSONAL NOTES

Remember: Laugh more!
Make the most of my time with my children.
They grow so fast!

A corner of this planner reserved for your own space; a place for jotting down a memory, a moment, a highlight that might otherwise be lost.

HIGHLIGHTS FOR THE MONTH OF _____

Sunday	Monday	Tuesday	Wednesday	Thursday	Friday	Saturday

Unscheduled items for this month: _____

BIRTHDAYS & ANNIVERSARIES

Date	Name	Family Traditions	Preparations
_____	_____	_____	_____
_____	_____	_____	_____
_____	_____	_____	_____
_____	_____	_____	_____

HOLIDAYS

_____	_____	_____	_____
_____	_____	_____	_____

SEED YOU WOULD LIKE TO DEVELOP THIS WEEK:

_____

PLANTING THE SEED

Plan daily actions that will help you produce the fruit you desire.

Self-Check

S	M	T	W	T	F	S
☐	☐	☐	☐	☐	☐	☐
☐	☐	☐	☐	☐	☐	☐
☐	☐	☐	☐	☐	☐	☐

WATERING THE SEED

Encouragement from God's Word. Inspiring thoughts. Helpful words from others.

Month of:	Sunday...........	Monday...........	Tuesday...........

DAILY APPOINTMENTS AND ACTIVITIES

REMINDERS FOR FAMILY AND HOME

PRAYER GARDEN

REAPING THE HARVEST

Fruit you are seeing in your life this week as a result of God's nurturing and your faithful efforts. *(Be sure to consider little changes.)*

_____
_____
_____
_____
_____
_____
_____

"Whatever you do, work at it with all your heart, as working for the Lord, not for men, since you know that you will receive an inheritance from the Lord as a reward."

Colossians 3:23, 24

Wednesday............

_____
_____
_____
_____
_____
_____
_____
_____
_____

_____
_____
_____

Thursday............

_____
_____
_____
_____
_____
_____
_____
_____
_____

_____
_____
_____

Friday............

_____
_____
_____
_____
_____
_____
_____
_____
_____

_____
_____
_____

Saturday............

_____
_____
_____
_____
_____
_____
_____
_____
_____

_____
_____
_____

PERSONAL NOTES

_____
_____
_____

SEED YOU WOULD LIKE TO DEVELOP THIS WEEK:

_____

Self-Check

S	M	T	W	T	F	S
☐	☐	☐	☐	☐	☐	☐
☐	☐	☐	☐	☐	☐	☐
☐	☐	☐	☐	☐	☐	☐

PLANTING THE SEED

Plan daily actions that will help you produce the fruit you desire.

_____
_____
_____

WATERING THE SEED

Encouragement from God's Word. Inspiring thoughts. Helpful words from others.

_____
_____
_____

Month of:

_____

DAILY APPOINTMENTS AND ACTIVITIES

Sunday............	Monday............	Tuesday............
_____	_____	_____
_____	_____	_____
_____	_____	_____
_____	_____	_____
_____	_____	_____
_____	_____	_____
_____	_____	_____
_____	_____	_____
_____	_____	_____
_____	_____	_____
_____	_____	_____
_____	_____	_____

REMINDERS FOR FAMILY AND HOME

_____	_____	_____
_____	_____	_____
_____	_____	_____

PRAYER GARDEN

_____
_____
_____

REAPING THE HARVEST

Fruit you are seeing in your life this week as a result of God's nurturing and your faithful efforts. *(Be sure to consider little changes.)*

_____
_____
_____
_____
_____
_____
_____

"But remember the Lord your God, for it is he who gives you the ability to produce wealth."

Deuteronomy 8:18

Wednesday............

Thursday............

Friday............

Saturday............

PERSONAL NOTES

SEED YOU WOULD LIKE TO DEVELOP THIS WEEK:

_____

PLANTING THE SEED — Plan daily actions that will help you produce the fruit you desire.

Self-Check

S	M	T	W	T	F	S
☐	☐	☐	☐	☐	☐	☐
☐	☐	☐	☐	☐	☐	☐
☐	☐	☐	☐	☐	☐	☐

WATERING THE SEED — Encouragement from God's Word. Inspiring thoughts. Helpful words from others.

_____

_____

_____

Month of: _____

	Sunday............	Monday............	Tuesday............

DAILY APPOINTMENTS AND ACTIVITIES

REMINDERS FOR FAMILY AND HOME

PRAYER GARDEN

REAPING THE HARVEST

Fruit you are seeing in your life this week as a result of God's nurturing and your faithful efforts. *(Be sure to consider little changes.)*

_____
_____
_____
_____
_____
_____
_____

"But the wisdom that comes from heaven is first of all pure; then peace loving, considerate, submissive, full of mercy and good fruit impartial and sincere."

James 3:17

Wednesday...........

Thursday...........

Friday...........

Saturday...........

PERSONAL NOTES

SEED YOU WOULD LIKE TO DEVELOP THIS WEEK:

PLANTING THE SEED

Plan daily actions that will help you produce the fruit you desire.

WATERING THE SEED

Encouragement from God's Word. Inspiring thoughts. Helpful words from others.

Month of:	Sunday...........	Monday...........	Tuesday...........
DAILY APPOINTMENTS AND ACTIVITIES			

REMINDERS FOR FAMILY AND HOME

PRAYER GARDEN

REAPING THE HARVEST

Fruit you are seeing in your life this week as a result of God's nurturing and your faithful efforts. *(Be sure to consider little changes.)*

_____
_____
_____
_____
_____
_____

"You care for the land and water it; you enrich it abundantly. The streams of God are filled with water to provide the people with grain, for so you have ordained it."

Psalms 65:9

Wednesday............	Thursday............	Friday............	Saturday............

PERSONAL NOTES

SEED YOU WOULD LIKE TO DEVELOP THIS WEEK:

_____

	S	M	T	W	T	F	S

PLANTING THE SEED

Plan daily actions that will help you produce the fruit you desire.

_____

_____

_____

WATERING THE SEED

Encouragement from God's Word. Inspiring thoughts. Helpful words from others.

_____

_____

_____

Month of:

_____

DAILY APPOINTMENTS AND ACTIVITIES

Sunday............	Monday............	Tuesday............

REMINDERS FOR FAMILY AND HOME

PRAYER GARDEN

_____

_____

_____

REAPING THE HARVEST

Fruit you are seeing in your life this week as a result of God's nurturing and your faithful efforts. *(Be sure to consider little changes.)*

_____
_____
_____
_____
_____
_____
_____

"You crown the year with your bounty, and your carts overflow with abundance."

Psalm 65:11

Wednesday............

Thursday............

Friday............

Saturday............

PERSONAL NOTES

A *corner of this planner reserved for your own space; a place for jotting down a memory, a moment, a highlight that might otherwise be lost.*

Highlights for the Month of _____

Sunday	Monday	Tuesday	Wednesday	Thursday	Friday	Saturday

Unscheduled items for this month: _____

Birthdays & Anniversaries

Date	Name	Family Traditions	Preparations
_____	_____	_____	_____
_____	_____	_____	_____
_____	_____	_____	_____
_____	_____	_____	_____

Holidays

_____	_____	_____	_____
_____	_____	_____	_____

SEED YOU WOULD LIKE TO DEVELOP THIS WEEK:

_____

PLANTING THE SEED

Plan daily actions that will help you produce the fruit you desire.

Self-Check

S	M	T	W	T	F	S
☐	☐	☐	☐	☐	☐	☐
☐	☐	☐	☐	☐	☐	☐
☐	☐	☐	☐	☐	☐	☐

_____

_____

_____

WATERING THE SEED

Encouragement from God's Word. Inspiring thoughts. Helpful words from others.

_____

_____

_____

Month of:

_____

DAILY APPOINTMENTS AND ACTIVITIES

Sunday...........

Monday...........

Tuesday...........

REMINDERS FOR FAMILY AND HOME

PRAYER GARDEN

REAPING THE HARVEST

Fruit you are seeing in your life this week as a result of God's nurturing and your faithful efforts. *(Be sure to consider little changes.)*

_____
_____
_____
_____
_____
_____
_____

"The Lord will open the heavens, the storehouse of his bounty, to send rain on your land in season and to bless all the work of your hands."

Deuteronomy 28:12

Wednesday............

_____
_____
_____
_____
_____
_____
_____
_____
_____

Thursday............

_____
_____
_____
_____
_____
_____
_____
_____
_____

Friday............

_____
_____
_____
_____
_____
_____
_____
_____
_____

Saturday............

_____
_____
_____
_____
_____
_____
_____
_____
_____

PERSONAL NOTES

_____
_____
_____

SEED YOU WOULD LIKE TO DEVELOP THIS WEEK:

_____

PLANTING THE SEED

Plan daily actions that will help you produce the fruit you desire.

_____
_____
_____

Self-Check

S	M	T	W	T	F	S
☐	☐	☐	☐	☐	☐	☐
☐	☐	☐	☐	☐	☐	☐
☐	☐	☐	☐	☐	☐	☐

WATERING THE SEED

Encouragement from God's Word. Inspiring thoughts. Helpful words from others.

_____
_____
_____

Month of: _____

_____

DAILY APPOINTMENTS AND ACTIVITIES

Sunday............

_____
_____
_____
_____
_____
_____
_____
_____
_____
_____

Monday............

_____
_____
_____
_____
_____
_____
_____
_____
_____
_____

Tuesday............

_____
_____
_____
_____
_____
_____
_____
_____
_____
_____

REMINDERS FOR FAMILY AND HOME

_____
_____

_____
_____

_____
_____

PRAYER GARDEN

_____
_____

REAPING THE HARVEST

Fruit you are seeing in your life this week as a result of God's nurturing and your faithful efforts.
(Be sure to consider little changes.)

_____
_____
_____
_____
_____
_____

"Sow for yourselves righteousness, reap the fruit of unfailing love, and break up your unplowed ground for it is time to seek the Lord, until he comes and showers righteousness on you."

Hosea 10:12

Wednesday...........	Thursday...........	Friday...........	Saturday...........

PERSONAL NOTES

SEED YOU WOULD LIKE TO DEVELOP THIS WEEK:

_____

PLANTING THE SEED

Plan daily actions that will help you produce the fruit you desire.

_____

_____

_____

S	M	T	W	T	F	S
☐	☐	☐	☐	☐	☐	☐
☐	☐	☐	☐	☐	☐	☐
☐	☐	☐	☐	☐	☐	☐

WATERING THE SEED

Encouragement from God's Word. Inspiring thoughts. Helpful words from others.

_____

_____

_____

Month of:

_____

DAILY APPOINTMENTS AND ACTIVITIES

Sunday............	Monday............	Tuesday............

REMINDERS FOR FAMILY AND HOME

PRAYER GARDEN

REAPING THE HARVEST

Fruit you are seeing in your life this week as a result of God's nurturing and your faithful efforts. *(Be sure to consider little changes.)*

_____
_____
_____
_____
_____
_____
_____

"Remember this: Whosoever sows sparingly will also reap sparingly, and whosoever sows generously will also reap generously."

2 Corinthians 9:6

Wednesday...........

Thursday...........

Friday...........

Saturday...........

PERSONAL NOTES

SEED YOU WOULD LIKE TO DEVELOP THIS WEEK:

_____

PLANTING THE SEED

Plan daily actions that will help you produce the fruit you desire.

Self-Check

S	M	T	W	T	F	S
☐	☐	☐	☐	☐	☐	☐
☐	☐	☐	☐	☐	☐	☐
☐	☐	☐	☐	☐	☐	☐

WATERING THE SEED

Encouragement from God's Word. Inspiring thoughts. Helpful words from others.

_____

Month of:

_____

DAILY APPOINTMENTS AND ACTIVITIES

Sunday...........

Monday...........

Tuesday...........

REMINDERS FOR FAMILY AND HOME

PRAYER GARDEN

REAPING
THE
HARVEST

Fruit you are seeing in your life this week as a result of God's nurturing and your faithful efforts. *(Be sure to consider little changes.)*

_____
_____
_____
_____
_____
_____
_____

"She gets up while it is still dark; she provides food for her family and portions for servant girls."

Proverbs 31:15

Wednesday............

_____
_____
_____
_____
_____
_____
_____
_____
_____
_____

Thursday............

_____
_____
_____
_____
_____
_____
_____
_____
_____
_____

Friday............

_____
_____
_____
_____
_____
_____
_____
_____
_____
_____

Saturday............

_____
_____
_____
_____
_____
_____
_____
_____
_____
_____

_____   _____   _____   _____
_____   _____   _____   _____
_____   _____   _____   _____

PERSONAL
NOTES

_____
_____
_____

SEED YOU WOULD LIKE TO DEVELOP THIS WEEK:

_____

PLANTING THE SEED

Plan daily actions that will help you produce the fruit you desire.

_____

_____

_____

WATERING THE SEED

Encouragement from God's Word. Inspiring thoughts. Helpful words from others.

_____

_____

_____

Month of: _____

Sunday............   Monday............   Tuesday............

DAILY APPOINTMENTS AND ACTIVITIES

REMINDERS FOR FAMILY AND HOME

PRAYER GARDEN

REAPING THE HARVEST

Fruit you are seeing in your life this week as a result of God's nurturing and your faithful efforts.
(Be sure to consider little changes.)

_____
_____
_____
_____
_____
_____
_____

"Make it your ambition to lead a quiet life, to mind your own business and to work with your hands, just as we told you, so that your daily life may win the respect of outsiders..."

1 Thessalonians 4:11,12

Wednesday...........	Thursday...........	Friday...........	Saturday...........

PERSONAL NOTES

_____
_____
_____

A corner of this planner reserved for your own space; a place for jotting down a memory, a moment, a highlight that might otherwise be lost.

HIGHLIGHTS FOR THE MONTH OF _____

Sunday	Monday	Tuesday	Wednesday	Thursday	Friday	Saturday

Unscheduled items for this month: _____

BIRTHDAYS & ANNIVERSARIES

Date	Name	Family Traditions	Preparations
_____	_____	_____	_____
_____	_____	_____	_____
_____	_____	_____	_____
_____	_____	_____	_____
_____	_____	_____	_____

HOLIDAYS

_____

_____

SEED YOU WOULD LIKE TO DEVELOP THIS WEEK:

_____

PLANTING THE SEED — Plan daily actions that will help you produce the fruit you desire.

_____

_____

_____

Self-Check

S	M	T	W	T	F	S
☐	☐	☐	☐	☐	☐	☐
☐	☐	☐	☐	☐	☐	☐
☐	☐	☐	☐	☐	☐	☐

WATERING THE SEED — Encouragement from God's Word. Inspiring thoughts. Helpful words from others.

_____

_____

Month of:

_____

DAILY APPOINTMENTS AND ACTIVITIES

Sunday............	Monday............	Tuesday............

REMINDERS FOR FAMILY AND HOME

PRAYER GARDEN

REAPING THE HARVEST

Fruit you are seeing in your life this week as a result of God's nurturing and your faithful efforts. *(Be sure to consider little changes.)*

_____
_____
_____
_____
_____
_____
_____

"He who gathers crops in summer is a wise son, but he who sleeps during harvest is a disgraceful son."

Proverbs 10:5

Wednesday............

Thursday............

Friday............

Saturday............

PERSONAL NOTES

SEED YOU WOULD LIKE TO DEVELOP THIS WEEK:

_____

PLANTING THE SEED

Plan daily actions that will help you produce the fruit you desire.

Self-Check

S	M	T	W	T	F	S
☐	☐	☐	☐	☐	☐	☐
☐	☐	☐	☐	☐	☐	☐
☐	☐	☐	☐	☐	☐	☐

WATERING THE SEED

Encouragement from God's Word. Inspiring thoughts. Helpful words from others.

Month of:	Sunday............	Monday............	Tuesday............
DAILY APPOINTMENTS AND ACTIVITIES			

REMINDERS FOR FAMILY AND HOME

PRAYER GARDEN

REAPING THE HARVEST

Fruit you are seeing in your life this week as a result of God's nurturing and your faithful efforts. *(Be sure to consider little changes.)*

_____
_____
_____
_____
_____
_____
_____

"Produce fruit in keeping with repentance."

Matthew 3:8

Wednesday............

_____
_____
_____
_____
_____
_____
_____
_____
_____
_____
_____

_____
_____
_____

Thursday............

_____
_____
_____
_____
_____
_____
_____
_____
_____
_____
_____

_____
_____
_____

Friday............

_____
_____
_____
_____
_____
_____
_____
_____
_____
_____
_____

_____
_____
_____

Saturday............

_____
_____
_____
_____
_____
_____
_____
_____
_____
_____
_____

_____
_____
_____

PERSONAL NOTES

_____
_____
_____

SEED YOU WOULD LIKE TO DEVELOP THIS WEEK:

_____

PLANTING THE SEED

Plan daily actions that will help you produce the fruit you desire.

WATERING THE SEED

Encouragement from God's Word. Inspiring thoughts. Helpful words from others.

Self-Check

S	M	T	W	T	F	S
☐	☐	☐	☐	☐	☐	☐
☐	☐	☐	☐	☐	☐	☐
☐	☐	☐	☐	☐	☐	☐

Month of: _____

Sunday.............   Monday.............   Tuesday.............

DAILY APPOINTMENTS AND ACTIVITIES

REMINDERS FOR FAMILY AND HOME

PRAYER GARDEN

REAPING THE HARVEST

Fruit you are seeing in your life this week as a result of God's nurturing and your faithful efforts. *(Be sure to consider little changes.)*

_____
_____
_____
_____
_____
_____

"So that you may be able to discern what is best and may be pure, and blameless...filled with the fruit of righteousness that comes through Jesus Christ—to the glory and praise of God."

Philippians 1:10,11

Wednesday...........

Thursday...........

Friday...........

Saturday...........

PERSONAL NOTES

SEED YOU WOULD LIKE TO DEVELOP THIS WEEK:

_____

PLANTING THE SEED

Plan daily actions that will help you produce the fruit you desire.

_____

_____

_____

Self-Check

S	M	T	W	T	F	S
☐	☐	☐	☐	☐	☐	☐
☐	☐	☐	☐	☐	☐	☐
☐	☐	☐	☐	☐	☐	☐

WATERING THE SEED

Encouragement from God's Word. Inspiring thoughts. Helpful words from others.

_____

_____

_____

Month of:

_____

	Sunday...........	Monday...........	Tuesday...........

DAILY APPOINTMENTS AND ACTIVITIES

REMINDERS FOR FAMILY AND HOME

PRAYER GARDEN

REAPING THE HARVEST

Fruit you are seeing in your life this week as a result of God's nurturing and your faithful efforts. *(Be sure to consider little changes.)*

_____
_____
_____
_____
_____
_____
_____

"Still other seed fell on good soil, where it produced a crop–a hundred, sixty or thirty times what was sown."

Matthew 3:18

Wednesday...........

_____
_____
_____
_____
_____
_____
_____
_____
_____
_____

_____
_____
_____

Thursday...........

_____
_____
_____
_____
_____
_____
_____
_____
_____
_____

_____
_____
_____

Friday...........

_____
_____
_____
_____
_____
_____
_____
_____
_____
_____

_____
_____
_____

Saturday...........

_____
_____
_____
_____
_____
_____
_____
_____
_____
_____

_____
_____
_____

PERSONAL NOTES

_____
_____
_____

SEED YOU WOULD LIKE TO DEVELOP THIS WEEK:

_____

PLANTING THE SEED

Plan daily actions that will help you produce the fruit you desire.

WATERING THE SEED

Encouragement from God's Word. Inspiring thoughts. Helpful words from others.

Self-Check

S	M	T	W	T	F	S
☐	☐	☐	☐	☐	☐	☐
☐	☐	☐	☐	☐	☐	☐
☐	☐	☐	☐	☐	☐	☐

Month of: _____

DAILY APPOINTMENTS AND ACTIVITIES

Sunday............

Monday............

Tuesday............

REMINDERS FOR FAMILY AND HOME

PRAYER GARDEN

REAPING THE HARVEST

Fruit you are seeing in your life this week as a result of God's nurturing and your faithful efforts. *(Be sure to consider little changes.)*

_____
_____
_____
_____
_____
_____

"He [the gardener] cuts off every branch in me that bears no fruit, while every branch that does bear fruit he trims clean so that it will be even more fruitful."

John 15:2

Wednesday...........	Thursday...........	Friday...........	Saturday...........

PERSONAL NOTES

A corner of this planner reserved for your own space; a place for jotting down a memory, a moment, a highlight that might otherwise be lost.

Sunday	Monday	Tuesday	Wednesday	Thursday	Friday	Saturday

Unscheduled items for this month: _____

BIRTHDAYS & ANNIVERSARIES

Date	Name	Family Traditions	Preparations
_____	_____	_____	_____
_____	_____	_____	_____
_____	_____	_____	_____
_____	_____	_____	_____

HOLIDAYS

_____	_____	_____	_____
_____	_____	_____	_____

SEED YOU WOULD LIKE TO DEVELOP THIS WEEK:

_____

PLANTING THE SEED

Plan daily actions that will help you produce the fruit you desire.

_____

_____

_____

WATERING THE SEED

Encouragement from God's Word. Inspiring thoughts. Helpful words from others.

_____

_____

_____

Month of: _____

DAILY APPOINTMENTS AND ACTIVITIES

Sunday............

Monday............

Tuesday............

REMINDERS FOR FAMILY AND HOME

PRAYER GARDEN

REAPING THE HARVEST

Fruit you are seeing in your life this week as a result of God's nurturing and your faithful efforts. *(Be sure to consider little changes.)*

_____
_____
_____
_____
_____
_____
_____

"No discipline seems pleasant at the time, but painful. Later on, however, it produces a harvest of righteousness and peace for those who have been trained by it."

Hebrews 12:11

Wednesday............

Thursday............

Friday............

Saturday............

PERSONAL NOTES

SEED YOU WOULD LIKE TO DEVELOP THIS WEEK:

	S	M	T	W	T	F	S

PLANTING THE SEED
Plan daily actions that will help you produce the fruit you desire.

WATERING THE SEED
Encouragement from God's Word. Inspiring thoughts. Helpful words from others.

Month of: _____

DAILY APPOINTMENTS AND ACTIVITIES

	Sunday............	Monday............	Tuesday............

REMINDERS FOR FAMILY AND HOME

PRAYER GARDEN

REAPING THE HARVEST

Fruit you are seeing in your life this week as a result of God's nurturing and your faithful efforts. *(Be sure to consider little changes.)*

_____
_____
_____
_____
_____
_____

"Let us not become weary in doing good, for at the proper time we will reap a harvest if we do not give up."

Galatians 6:9

Wednesday............	Thursday............	Friday............	Saturday............

PERSONAL NOTES

SEED YOU WOULD LIKE TO DEVELOP THIS WEEK:

_____

PLANTING THE SEED

Plan daily actions that will help you produce the fruit you desire.

Self-Check

S	M	T	W	T	F	S
☐	☐	☐	☐	☐	☐	☐
☐	☐	☐	☐	☐	☐	☐
☐	☐	☐	☐	☐	☐	☐

WATERING THE SEED

Encouragement from God's Word. Inspiring thoughts. Helpful words from others.

_____

_____

Month of: _____ Sunday............ Monday............ Tuesday............

DAILY APPOINTMENTS AND ACTIVITIES

REMINDERS FOR FAMILY AND HOME

PRAYER GARDEN

REAPING
THE
HARVEST

Fruit you are
seeing in your life
this week as a
result of God's
nurturing and your
faithful efforts.
*(Be sure to consider
little changes.)*

_____
_____
_____
_____
_____
_____

"Peacemakers who sow in peace
raise a harvest of righteousness."
James 3:18

Wednesday............

_____
_____
_____
_____
_____
_____
_____
_____
_____
_____
_____

_____
_____

Thursday............

_____
_____
_____
_____
_____
_____
_____
_____
_____
_____
_____

_____
_____

Friday............

_____
_____
_____
_____
_____
_____
_____
_____
_____
_____
_____

_____
_____

Saturday............

_____
_____
_____
_____
_____
_____
_____
_____
_____
_____
_____

_____
_____

PERSONAL
NOTES

_____
_____
_____

SEED YOU WOULD LIKE TO DEVELOP THIS WEEK:

_____

PLANTING THE SEED

Plan daily actions that will help you produce the fruit you desire.

_____

_____

_____

WATERING THE SEED

Encouragement from God's Word. Inspiring thoughts. Helpful words from others.

_____

_____

_____

Month of: _____

Sunday............

Monday............

Tuesday............

DAILY APPOINTMENTS AND ACTIVITIES

REMINDERS FOR FAMILY AND HOME

PRAYER GARDEN

REAPING THE HARVEST

Fruit you are seeing in your life this week as a result of God's nurturing and your faithful efforts.
(Be sure to consider little changes.)

_____
_____
_____
_____
_____
_____
_____
_____

"Now he who supplies seed to the sower and bread for food will also supply and increase your store of seed and will enlarge the harvest of your righteousness."

2 Corinthians 9:10

Wednesday............

_____
_____
_____
_____
_____
_____
_____
_____
_____
_____
_____

_____
_____
_____

Thursday............

_____
_____
_____
_____
_____
_____
_____
_____
_____
_____
_____

_____
_____
_____

Friday............

_____
_____
_____
_____
_____
_____
_____
_____
_____
_____
_____

_____
_____
_____

Saturday............

_____
_____
_____
_____
_____
_____
_____
_____
_____
_____
_____

_____
_____
_____

PERSONAL NOTES

_____
_____
_____

SEED YOU WOULD LIKE TO DEVELOP THIS WEEK:

_____

S	M	T	W	T	F	S
☐	☐	☐	☐	☐	☐	☐
☐	☐	☐	☐	☐	☐	☐
☐	☐	☐	☐	☐	☐	☐

PLANTING THE SEED

Plan daily actions that will help you produce the fruit you desire.

_____
_____
_____

WATERING THE SEED

Encouragement from God's Word. Inspiring thoughts. Helpful words from others.

_____
_____
_____

Month of:

_____

DAILY APPOINTMENTS AND ACTIVITIES

Sunday..........	Monday..........	Tuesday..........
_____	_____	_____
_____	_____	_____
_____	_____	_____
_____	_____	_____
_____	_____	_____
_____	_____	_____
_____	_____	_____
_____	_____	_____
_____	_____	_____
_____	_____	_____
_____	_____	_____

REMINDERS FOR FAMILY AND HOME

_____	_____	_____
_____	_____	_____

PRAYER GARDEN

_____
_____
_____

REAPING THE HARVEST

Fruit you are seeing in your life this week as a result of God's nurturing and your faithful efforts. *(Be sure to consider little changes.)*

_____
_____
_____
_____
_____
_____

"He who tends a fig tree will eat its fruit, and he who looks after his master will be honored."

Proverbs 27:18

Wednesday............	Thursday............	Friday............	Saturday............

PERSONAL NOTES

A corner of this planner reserved for your own space; a place for jotting down a memory, a moment, a highlight that might otherwise be lost.

HIGHLIGHTS FOR THE MONTH OF _____

Sunday	Monday	Tuesday	Wednesday	Thursday	Friday	Saturday

Unscheduled items for this month: _____

BIRTHDAYS & ANNIVERSARIES

Date	Name	Family Traditions	Preparations
_____	_____	_____	_____
_____	_____	_____	_____
_____	_____	_____	_____
_____	_____	_____	_____

HOLIDAYS

_____	_____	_____	_____
_____	_____	_____	_____

SEED YOU WOULD LIKE TO DEVELOP THIS WEEK:

_____

	S	M	T	W	T	F	S
	☐	☐	☐	☐	☐	☐	☐
	☐	☐	☐	☐	☐	☐	☐
	☐	☐	☐	☐	☐	☐	☐

PLANTING THE SEED
Plan daily actions that will help you produce the fruit you desire.

_____

_____

_____

WATERING THE SEED
Encouragement from God's Word. Inspiring thoughts. Helpful words from others.

_____

_____

_____

Month of:	Sunday............	Monday............	Tuesday............
DAILY APPOINTMENTS AND ACTIVITIES			

REMINDERS FOR FAMILY AND HOME

PRAYER GARDEN

REAPING THE HARVEST

Fruit you are seeing in your life this week as a result of God's nurturing and your faithful efforts. *(Be sure to consider little changes.)*

_____
_____
_____
_____
_____
_____
_____

"Whoever has will be given more, and he will have an abundance. Whoever does not have, even what he has will be taken from him."

Matthew 13:12

Wednesday............	Thursday............	Friday............	Saturday............

PERSONAL NOTES

SEED YOU WOULD LIKE TO DEVELOP THIS WEEK:

_____

PLANTING THE SEED

Plan daily actions that will help you produce the fruit you desire.

_____

_____

_____

Self-Check

S	M	T	W	T	F	S
☐	☐	☐	☐	☐	☐	☐
☐	☐	☐	☐	☐	☐	☐
☐	☐	☐	☐	☐	☐	☐

WATERING THE SEED

Encouragement from God's Word. Inspiring thoughts. Helpful words from others.

_____

_____

_____

Month of:

Sunday............   Monday............   Tuesday............

_____

DAILY APPOINTMENTS AND ACTIVITIES

REMINDERS FOR FAMILY AND HOME

PRAYER GARDEN

REAPING THE HARVEST

Fruit you are seeing in your life this week as a result of God's nurturing and your faithful efforts. *(Be sure to consider little changes.)*

_____
_____
_____
_____
_____
_____
_____

"He who works his land will have abundant food, but the one who chases fantasies will have his fill of poverty."

Proverbs 28:19

Wednesday............

_____
_____
_____
_____
_____
_____
_____
_____
_____
_____

_____
_____
_____

Thursday............

_____
_____
_____
_____
_____
_____
_____
_____
_____
_____

_____
_____
_____

Friday............

_____
_____
_____
_____
_____
_____
_____
_____
_____
_____

_____
_____

Saturday............

_____
_____
_____
_____
_____
_____
_____
_____
_____
_____

_____
_____
_____

PERSONAL NOTES

_____
_____
_____

Seed You Would Like to Develop This Week:

_____

Planting the Seed

Plan daily actions that will help you produce the fruit you desire.

Self-Check

S	M	T	W	T	F	S
☐	☐	☐	☐	☐	☐	☐
☐	☐	☐	☐	☐	☐	☐
☐	☐	☐	☐	☐	☐	☐

_____
_____
_____

Watering the Seed

Encouragement from God's Word. Inspiring thoughts. Helpful words from others.

_____
_____
_____

Month of:

_____

Sunday........... Monday........... Tuesday...........

Daily Appointments and Activities

Reminders for Family and Home

Prayer Garden

REAPING THE HARVEST

Fruit you are seeing in your life this week as a result of God's nurturing and your faithful efforts. *(Be sure to consider little changes.)*

_____
_____
_____
_____
_____
_____
_____

"Remain in me, and I will remain in you. No branch can bear fruit by itself; it must remain in the vine. Neither can you bear fruit unless you remain in me."

John 15:4

Wednesday............

Thursday............

Friday............

Saturday............

PERSONAL NOTES

SEED YOU WOULD LIKE TO DEVELOP THIS WEEK:

_____

_____

S	M	T	W	T	F	S
☐	☐	☐	☐	☐	☐	☐
☐	☐	☐	☐	☐	☐	☐
☐	☐	☐	☐	☐	☐	☐

PLANTING THE SEED
Plan daily actions that will help you produce the fruit you desire.

_____

_____

_____

WATERING THE SEED
Encouragement from God's Word. Inspiring thoughts. Helpful words from others.

_____

_____

_____

Month of:	Sunday............	Monday............	Tuesday............

DAILY APPOINTMENTS AND ACTIVITIES

REMINDERS FOR FAMILY AND HOME

PRAYER GARDEN

REAPING THE HARVEST

Fruit you are seeing in your life this week as a result of God's nurturing and your faithful efforts. *(Be sure to consider little changes.)*

_____
_____
_____
_____
_____
_____
_____

"I am the vine; you are the branches. If a man remains in me and I in him, he will bear much fruit; apart from me you can do nothing."

John 15:5

Wednesday............	Thursday............	Friday............	Saturday............

PERSONAL NOTES

SEED YOU WOULD LIKE TO DEVELOP THIS WEEK:

_____

Self-Check

	S	M	T	W	T	F	S
PLANTING THE SEED — Plan daily actions that will help you produce the fruit you desire.	☐	☐	☐	☐	☐	☐	☐
	☐	☐	☐	☐	☐	☐	☐
	☐	☐	☐	☐	☐	☐	☐

PLANTING THE SEED — Plan daily actions that will help you produce the fruit you desire.

_____

_____

_____

WATERING THE SEED — Encouragement from God's Word. Inspiring thoughts. Helpful words from others.

_____

_____

_____

Month of: _____

Sunday............   Monday............   Tuesday............

DAILY APPOINTMENTS AND ACTIVITIES

REMINDERS FOR FAMILY AND HOME

PRAYER GARDEN

REAPING THE HARVEST

Fruit you are seeing in your life this week as a result of God's nurturing and your faithful efforts.
(Be sure to consider little changes.)

_____
_____
_____
_____
_____
_____
_____

"May the favor of the Lord our God rest upon us; establish the work of our hands for us—yes, establish the work of our hands."

Psalm 90:17

Wednesday...........

Thursday...........

Friday...........

Saturday...........

PERSONAL NOTES

A *corner of this planner reserved for your own space; a place for jotting down a memory, a moment, a highlight that might otherwise be lost.*

HIGHLIGHTS FOR THE MONTH OF _____

Sunday	Monday	Tuesday	Wednesday	Thursday	Friday	Saturday

Unscheduled items for this month: _____

BIRTHDAYS & ANNIVERSARIES

Date	Name	Family Traditions	Preparations
_____	_____	_____	_____
_____	_____	_____	_____
_____	_____	_____	_____
_____	_____	_____	_____

HOLIDAYS

_____	_____	_____	_____
_____	_____	_____	_____

SEED YOU WOULD LIKE TO DEVELOP THIS WEEK:

_____

S	M	T	W	T	F	S
☐	☐	☐	☐	☐	☐	☐
☐	☐	☐	☐	☐	☐	☐
☐	☐	☐	☐	☐	☐	☐

PLANTING THE SEED

Plan daily actions that will help you produce the fruit you desire.

_____

_____

_____

WATERING THE SEED

Encouragement from God's Word. Inspiring thoughts. Helpful words from others.

_____

_____

_____

Month of:

_____

DAILY APPOINTMENTS AND ACTIVITIES

Sunday............	Monday............	Tuesday............

REMINDERS FOR FAMILY AND HOME

PRAYER GARDEN

REAPING THE HARVEST

Fruit you are seeing in your life this week as a result of God's nurturing and your faithful efforts. *(Be sure to consider little changes.)*

_____
_____
_____
_____
_____
_____

"And whatever you do, whether in word or deed, do it all in the name of the Lord Jesus, giving thanks to God the Father through him."

Colossians 3:17

Wednesday...........	Thursday...........	Friday...........	Saturday...........

PERSONAL NOTES

_____
_____
_____

SEED YOU WOULD LIKE TO DEVELOP THIS WEEK:

_____

	S	M	T	W	T	F	S
	☐	☐	☐	☐	☐	☐	☐
	☐	☐	☐	☐	☐	☐	☐
	☐	☐	☐	☐	☐	☐	☐

PLANTING THE SEED
Plan daily actions that will help you produce the fruit you desire.

_____

_____

_____

WATERING THE SEED
Encouragement from God's Word. Inspiring thoughts. Helpful words from others.

_____

_____

_____

Month of: _____

DAILY APPOINTMENTS AND ACTIVITIES

Sunday............	Monday............	Tuesday............
_____	_____	_____
_____	_____	_____
_____	_____	_____
_____	_____	_____
_____	_____	_____
_____	_____	_____
_____	_____	_____
_____	_____	_____
_____	_____	_____
_____	_____	_____
_____	_____	_____

REMINDERS FOR FAMILY AND HOME

_____	_____	
_____	_____	
_____	_____	

PRAYER GARDEN

_____

_____

_____

REAPING THE HARVEST

Fruit you are seeing in your life this week as a result of God's nurturing and your faithful efforts. *(Be sure to consider little changes.)*

_____

_____

_____

_____

_____

_____

_____

"Tell the righteous it will be well with them, for they will enjoy the fruit of their deeds."

Isaiah 3:10

Wednesday............

_____
_____
_____
_____
_____
_____
_____
_____
_____

_____
_____
_____

Thursday............

_____
_____
_____
_____
_____
_____
_____
_____
_____

_____
_____
_____

Friday............

_____
_____
_____
_____
_____
_____
_____
_____
_____

_____
_____
_____

Saturday............

_____
_____
_____
_____
_____
_____
_____
_____
_____

_____
_____
_____

PERSONAL NOTES

_____

_____

_____

Self-Check

S	M	T	W	T	F	S
☐	☐	☐	☐	☐	☐	☐
☐	☐	☐	☐	☐	☐	☐
☐	☐	☐	☐	☐	☐	☐

PLANTING THE SEED
Plan daily actions that will help you produce the fruit you desire.

WATERING THE SEED
Encouragement from God's Word. Inspiring thoughts. Helpful words from others.

Month of:

Sunday...........   Monday...........   Tuesday...........

DAILY APPOINTMENTS AND ACTIVITIES

REMINDERS FOR FAMILY AND HOME

PRAYER GARDEN

REAPING THE HARVEST

Fruit you are seeing in your life this week as a result of God's nurturing and your faithful efforts. *(Be sure to consider little changes.)*

_____
_____
_____
_____
_____
_____
_____

"Being confident of this, that he who began a good work in you will carry it on to completion until the day of Christ Jesus."

Philippians 1:6

Wednesday............	Thursday............	Friday............	Saturday............

PERSONAL NOTES

SEED YOU WOULD LIKE TO DEVELOP THIS WEEK:

PLANTING THE SEED

Plan daily actions that will help you produce the fruit you desire.

Self-Check

S	M	T	W	T	F	S
☐	☐	☐	☐	☐	☐	☐
☐	☐	☐	☐	☐	☐	☐
☐	☐	☐	☐	☐	☐	☐

WATERING THE SEED

Encouragement from God's Word. Inspiring thoughts. Helpful words from others.

Month of:

DAILY APPOINTMENTS AND ACTIVITIES

Sunday............

Monday............

Tuesday............

REMINDERS FOR FAMILY AND HOME

PRAYER GARDEN

REAPING THE HARVEST

Fruit you are seeing in your life this week as a result of God's nurturing and your faithful efforts. *(Be sure to consider little changes.)*

_____

_____

_____

_____

_____

_____

_____

"For the Lord God will bless you in all your harvest and in all the work of your hands, and your joy will be complete."

Deuteronomy 16:15

Wednesday............

Thursday............

Friday............

Saturday............

PERSONAL NOTES

SEED YOU WOULD LIKE TO DEVELOP THIS WEEK:

PLANTING THE SEED
Plan daily actions that will help you produce the fruit you desire.

WATERING THE SEED
Encouragement from God's Word. Inspiring thoughts. Helpful words from others.

Month of:

Sunday............   Monday............   Tuesday............

DAILY APPOINTMENTS AND ACTIVITIES

REMINDERS FOR FAMILY AND HOME

PRAYER GARDEN

REAPING THE HARVEST

Fruit you are seeing in your life this week as a result of God's nurturing and your faithful efforts. *(Be sure to consider little changes.)*

_____
_____
_____
_____
_____
_____
_____

"The fruit of the righteous is a tree of life, and he who wins souls is wise."

Proverbs 11:30

Wednesday...........

Thursday...........

Friday...........

Saturday...........

PERSONAL NOTES

A *corner of this planner reserved for your own space; a place for jotting down a memory, a moment, a highlight that might otherwise be lost.*

HIGHLIGHTS FOR THE MONTH OF _____

Sunday	Monday	Tuesday	Wednesday	Thursday	Friday	Saturday

Unscheduled items for this month: _____

BIRTHDAYS & ANNIVERSARIES

Date	Name	Family Traditions	Preparations
_____	_____	_____	_____
_____	_____	_____	_____
_____	_____	_____	_____
_____	_____	_____	_____
_____	_____	_____	_____

HOLIDAYS

_____ _____ _____ _____

_____ _____ _____ _____

SEED YOU WOULD LIKE TO DEVELOP THIS WEEK:

_____

Self-Check

S	M	T	W	T	F	S
☐	☐	☐	☐	☐	☐	☐
☐	☐	☐	☐	☐	☐	☐
☐	☐	☐	☐	☐	☐	☐

PLANTING THE SEED

Plan daily actions that will help you produce the fruit you desire.

_____

_____

_____

WATERING THE SEED

Encouragement from God's Word. Inspiring thoughts. Helpful words from others.

_____

_____

_____

Month of:

_____

DAILY APPOINTMENTS AND ACTIVITIES

Sunday...........	Monday...........	Tuesday...........

REMINDERS FOR FAMILY AND HOME

PRAYER GARDEN

_____

_____

REAPING THE HARVEST

Fruit you are seeing in your life this week as a result of God's nurturing and your faithful efforts. *(Be sure to consider little changes.)*

_____
_____
_____
_____
_____
_____

"Sow for yourselves righteousness, reap the fruit of unfailing love, and break up your unplowed ground for it is time to seek the Lord, until he comes and showers righteousness on you."

Hosea 10:12

Wednesday...........

_____
_____
_____
_____
_____
_____
_____
_____
_____
_____

_____
_____

Thursday...........

_____
_____
_____
_____
_____
_____
_____
_____
_____
_____

_____
_____

Friday...........

_____
_____
_____
_____
_____
_____
_____
_____
_____
_____

_____
_____

Saturday...........

_____
_____
_____
_____
_____
_____
_____
_____
_____
_____

_____
_____

PERSONAL NOTES

_____
_____
_____
_____

SEED YOU WOULD LIKE TO DEVELOP THIS WEEK:

_____ Self-Check

	S	M	T	W	T	F	S

PLANTING THE SEED
Plan daily actions that will help you produce the fruit you desire.

_____ ☐ ☐ ☐ ☐ ☐ ☐ ☐
_____ ☐ ☐ ☐ ☐ ☐ ☐ ☐
_____ ☐ ☐ ☐ ☐ ☐ ☐ ☐

WATERING THE SEED
Encouragement from God's Word. Inspiring thoughts. Helpful words from others.

_____
_____
_____

Month of:	Sunday............	Monday............	Tuesday............
DAILY APPOINTMENTS AND ACTIVITIES			

REMINDERS FOR FAMILY AND HOME

PRAYER GARDEN

REAPING
THE
HARVEST

Fruit you are seeing in your life this week as a result of God's nurturing and your faithful efforts. *(Be sure to consider little changes.)*

_____
_____
_____
_____
_____
_____

"The fruit of righteousness will be peace; the effect of righteousness will be quietness and confidence forever."

Isaiah 32:17

Wednesday...........

_____
_____
_____
_____
_____
_____
_____
_____
_____
_____

_____
_____
_____

Thursday...........

_____
_____
_____
_____
_____
_____
_____
_____
_____
_____

_____
_____
_____

Friday...........

_____
_____
_____
_____
_____
_____
_____
_____
_____
_____

_____
_____
_____

Saturday...........

_____
_____
_____
_____
_____
_____
_____
_____
_____
_____

_____
_____
_____

PERSONAL
NOTES

_____
_____
_____

SEED YOU WOULD LIKE TO DEVELOP THIS WEEK:

_____

PLANTING THE SEED

Plan daily actions that will help you produce the fruit you desire.

_____

_____

_____

Self-Check

S	M	T	W	T	F	S
☐	☐	☐	☐	☐	☐	☐
☐	☐	☐	☐	☐	☐	☐
☐	☐	☐	☐	☐	☐	☐

WATERING THE SEED

Encouragement from God's Word. Inspiring thoughts. Helpful words from others.

_____

_____

_____

Month of:

Sunday...........

Monday...........

Tuesday...........

_____

DAILY APPOINTMENTS AND ACTIVITIES

REMINDERS FOR FAMILY AND HOME

PRAYER GARDEN

REAPING THE HARVEST

Fruit you are seeing in your life this week as a result of God's nurturing and your faithful efforts.
(Be sure to consider little changes.)

_____

_____

_____

_____

_____

_____

"God is able to make all grace abound to you, so that in all things at all times, having all that you need, you will abound in every good work."

2 Corinthians 9:8

Wednesday............   Thursday............   Friday............   Saturday............

PERSONAL NOTES

SEED YOU WOULD LIKE TO DEVELOP THIS WEEK:

_____

PLANTING THE SEED
Plan daily actions that will help you produce the fruit you desire.

_____

_____

_____

WATERING THE SEED
Encouragement from God's Word. Inspiring thoughts. Helpful words from others.

_____

_____

_____

Month of:
_____

DAILY APPOINTMENTS AND ACTIVITIES

Sunday...........

Monday...........

Tuesday...........

REMINDERS FOR FAMILY AND HOME

PRAYER GARDEN

REAPING THE HARVEST

Fruit you are seeing in your life this week as a result of God's nurturing and your faithful efforts.
(Be sure to consider little changes.)

_____
_____
_____
_____
_____
_____
_____

"But the fruit of the Spirit is love, joy, peace, patience, kindness, goodness, faithfulness, gentleness and self-control. Against such things there is no law."

Galatians 5:22

Wednesday...........	Thursday...........	Friday...........	Saturday...........

PERSONAL NOTES

Seed You Would Like to Develop This Week:

Planting the Seed
Plan daily actions that will help you produce the fruit you desire.

Self-Check

S	M	T	W	T	F	S
☐	☐	☐	☐	☐	☐	☐
☐	☐	☐	☐	☐	☐	☐
☐	☐	☐	☐	☐	☐	☐

Watering the Seed
Encouragement from God's Word. Inspiring thoughts. Helpful words from others.

Month of:

Sunday...........   Monday...........   Tuesday...........

Daily Appointments and Activities

Reminders for Family and Home

Prayer Garden

REAPING THE HARVEST

Fruit you are seeing in your life this week as a result of God's nurturing and your faithful efforts. *(Be sure to consider little changes.)*

_____
_____
_____
_____
_____
_____
_____

"And we pray this in order that you may live a life worthy of the Lord and may please him in every way: bearing fruit in every good work, growing in the knowledge of God."

Colossians 1:10

Wednesday............	Thursday............	Friday............	Saturday............

PERSONAL NOTES

_____
_____
_____

A *corner of this planner reserved for your own space; a place for jotting down a memory, a moment, a highlight that might otherwise be lost.*

HIGHLIGHTS FOR THE MONTH OF _____

Sunday	Monday	Tuesday	Wednesday	Thursday	Friday	Saturday

Unscheduled items for this month: _____

BIRTHDAYS & ANNIVERSARIES

Date	Name	Family Traditions	Preparations
_____	_____	_____	_____
_____	_____	_____	_____
_____	_____	_____	_____
_____	_____	_____	_____

HOLIDAYS

_____	_____	_____	_____
_____	_____	_____	_____

SEED YOU WOULD LIKE TO DEVELOP THIS WEEK:

_____

	S	M	T	W	T	F	S

PLANTING THE SEED

Plan daily actions that will help you produce the fruit you desire.

_____

_____

_____

☐ ☐ ☐ ☐ ☐ ☐ ☐
☐ ☐ ☐ ☐ ☐ ☐ ☐
☐ ☐ ☐ ☐ ☐ ☐ ☐

WATERING THE SEED

Encouragement from God's Word. Inspiring thoughts. Helpful words from others.

_____

_____

_____

Month of:	Sunday............	Monday............	Tuesday............
DAILY APPOINTMENTS AND ACTIVITIES			

REMINDERS FOR FAMILY AND HOME

PRAYER GARDEN

REAPING THE HARVEST

Fruit you are seeing in your life this week as a result of God's nurturing and your faithful efforts. *(Be sure to consider little changes.)*

_____
_____
_____
_____
_____
_____
_____

"Honor the Lord with your wealth, with the firstfruits of all your crops; then your barns will be filled to overflowing."

Proverbs 3:9

Wednesday...........

_____
_____
_____
_____
_____
_____
_____
_____
_____
_____

_____
_____
_____

Thursday...........

_____
_____
_____
_____
_____
_____
_____
_____
_____
_____

_____
_____
_____

Friday...........

_____
_____
_____
_____
_____
_____
_____
_____
_____
_____

_____
_____
_____

Saturday...........

_____
_____
_____
_____
_____
_____
_____
_____
_____
_____

_____
_____
_____

PERSONAL NOTES

_____
_____
_____

SEED YOU WOULD LIKE TO DEVELOP THIS WEEK:

_____

PLANTING THE SEED

Plan daily actions that will help you produce the fruit you desire.

WATERING THE SEED

Encouragement from God's Word. Inspiring thoughts. Helpful words from others.

_____

_____

Month of: _____

	Sunday............	Monday............	Tuesday............

DAILY APPOINTMENTS AND ACTIVITIES

REMINDERS FOR FAMILY AND HOME

PRAYER GARDEN

_____

_____

_____

REAPING THE HARVEST

Fruit you are seeing in your life this week as a result of God's nurturing and your faithful efforts. *(Be sure to consider little changes.)*

_____
_____
_____
_____
_____
_____
_____

"All over the world this gospel is producing fruit and growing, just as it has been doing among you since the day you heard it."

Colossians 1:6

Wednesday...........	Thursday...........	Friday...........	Saturday...........

PERSONAL NOTES

_____
_____
_____

SEED YOU WOULD LIKE TO DEVELOP THIS WEEK:

_____

PLANTING THE SEED

Plan daily actions that will help you produce the fruit you desire.

Self-Check

S	M	T	W	T	F	S
☐	☐	☐	☐	☐	☐	☐
☐	☐	☐	☐	☐	☐	☐
☐	☐	☐	☐	☐	☐	☐

WATERING THE SEED

Encouragement from God's Word. Inspiring thoughts. Helpful words from others.

_____

Month of: _____

Sunday............   Monday............   Tuesday............

DAILY APPOINTMENTS AND ACTIVITIES

REMINDERS FOR FAMILY AND HOME

PRAYER GARDEN

REAPING THE HARVEST

Fruit you are seeing in your life this week as a result of God's nurturing and your faithful efforts. *(Be sure to consider little changes.)*

_____
_____
_____
_____
_____
_____
_____

"Make it your ambition to lead a quiet life, to mind your own business and to work with your hands."

1 Thessalonians 4:11

Wednesday............	Thursday............	Friday............	Saturday............

PERSONAL NOTES

SEED YOU WOULD LIKE TO DEVELOP THIS WEEK:

_____

PLANTING THE SEED

Plan daily actions that will help you produce the fruit you desire.

Self-Check

S	M	T	W	T	F	S
☐	☐	☐	☐	☐	☐	☐
☐	☐	☐	☐	☐	☐	☐
☐	☐	☐	☐	☐	☐	☐

_____
_____
_____

WATERING THE SEED

Encouragement from God's Word. Inspiring thoughts. Helpful words from others.

_____
_____
_____

Month of: _____

DAILY APPOINTMENTS AND ACTIVITIES

Sunday............	Monday............	Tuesday............

REMINDERS FOR FAMILY AND HOME

PRAYER GARDEN

_____
_____

REAPING THE HARVEST

Fruit you are seeing in your life this week as a result of God's nurturing and your faithful efforts.
(Be sure to consider little changes.)

_____
_____
_____
_____
_____
_____
_____

"The man who plants and the man who waters have one purpose, and each will be rewarded according to his own labor."

1Corinthians 3:8

Wednesday...........	Thursday...........	Friday...........	Saturday...........

PERSONAL NOTES

SEED YOU WOULD LIKE TO DEVELOP THIS WEEK:

_____

PLANTING THE SEED

Plan daily actions that will help you produce the fruit you desire.

_____

_____

_____

S	M	T	W	T	F	S
☐	☐	☐	☐	☐	☐	☐
☐	☐	☐	☐	☐	☐	☐
☐	☐	☐	☐	☐	☐	☐

WATERING THE SEED

Encouragement from God's Word. Inspiring thoughts. Helpful words from others.

_____

_____

_____

Month of:

_____

DAILY APPOINTMENTS AND ACTIVITIES

Sunday............	Monday............	Tuesday............
_____	_____	_____
_____	_____	_____
_____	_____	_____
_____	_____	_____
_____	_____	_____
_____	_____	_____
_____	_____	_____
_____	_____	_____
_____	_____	_____
_____	_____	_____

REMINDERS FOR FAMILY AND HOME

_____	_____	_____
_____	_____	_____
_____	_____	_____

PRAYER GARDEN

_____

_____

_____

REAPING THE HARVEST

Fruit you are seeing in your life this week as a result of God's nurturing and your faithful efforts. *(Be sure to consider little changes.)*

_____
_____
_____
_____
_____
_____
_____

"You did not choose me, but I chose you to go and bear fruit–fruit that will last."

John 15:16

Wednesday............

Thursday............

Friday............

Saturday............

PERSONAL NOTES

A *corner of this planner reserved for your own space; a place for jotting down a memory, a moment, a highlight that might otherwise be lost.*

HIGHLIGHTS FOR THE MONTH OF _____

Sunday	Monday	Tuesday	Wednesday	Thursday	Friday	Saturday

Unscheduled items for this month: _____

BIRTHDAYS & ANNIVERSARIES

Date	Name	Family Traditions	Preparations
_____	_____	_____	_____
_____	_____	_____	_____
_____	_____	_____	_____
_____	_____	_____	_____

HOLIDAYS

_____	_____	_____	_____
_____	_____	_____	_____

SEED YOU WOULD LIKE TO DEVELOP THIS WEEK:

PLANTING THE SEED

Plan daily actions that will help you produce the fruit you desire.

Self-Check

S	M	T	W	T	F	S
☐	☐	☐	☐	☐	☐	☐
☐	☐	☐	☐	☐	☐	☐
☐	☐	☐	☐	☐	☐	☐

WATERING THE SEED

Encouragement from God's Word. Inspiring thoughts. Helpful words from others.

Month of:

	Sunday............	Monday............	Tuesday............

DAILY APPOINTMENTS AND ACTIVITIES

REMINDERS FOR FAMILY AND HOME

PRAYER GARDEN

REAPING
THE
HARVEST

Fruit you are seeing in your life this week as a result of God's nurturing and your faithful efforts. *(Be sure to consider little changes.)*

_____
_____
_____
_____
_____
_____
_____

"You will be like a well-watered garden, like a spring whose waters never fail."

Isaiah 58:11

Wednesday...........

Thursday...........

Friday...........

Saturday...........

PERSONAL
NOTES

SEED YOU WOULD LIKE TO DEVELOP THIS WEEK:

_____

PLANTING THE SEED

Plan daily actions that will help you produce the fruit you desire.

Self-Check

S	M	T	W	T	F	S
☐	☐	☐	☐	☐	☐	☐
☐	☐	☐	☐	☐	☐	☐
☐	☐	☐	☐	☐	☐	☐

_____

_____

_____

WATERING THE SEED

Encouragement from God's Word. Inspiring thoughts. Helpful words from others.

_____

_____

_____

Month of: _____   Sunday............   Monday............   Tuesday............

DAILY APPOINTMENTS AND ACTIVITIES

REMINDERS FOR FAMILY AND HOME

PRAYER GARDEN

REAPING THE HARVEST

Fruit you are seeing in your life this week as a result of God's nurturing and your faithful efforts. *(Be sure to consider little changes.)*

_____
_____
_____
_____
_____
_____
_____

"As long as the earth endures, seedtime and harvest, cold and heat, summer and winter, day and night will never cease."

Genesis 8:22

Wednesday...........	Thursday...........	Friday...........	Saturday...........

PERSONAL NOTES

_____
_____
_____

Seed You Would Like to Develop This Week:

Planting the Seed
Plan daily actions that will help you produce the fruit you desire.

Self-Check

S	M	T	W	T	F	S
☐	☐	☐	☐	☐	☐	☐
☐	☐	☐	☐	☐	☐	☐
☐	☐	☐	☐	☐	☐	☐

Watering the Seed
Encouragement from God's Word. Inspiring thoughts. Helpful words from others.

Month of:

Sunday............ Monday............ Tuesday............

Daily Appointments and Activities

Reminders for Family and Home

Prayer Garden

REAPING THE HARVEST

Fruit you are seeing in your life this week as a result of God's nurturing and your faithful efforts. *(Be sure to consider little changes.)*

_____
_____
_____
_____
_____
_____
_____

"Trust in the Lord forever, for the Lord, the Lord, is the Rock eternal."

Isaiah 26:4

Wednesday...........

Thursday...........

Friday...........

Saturday...........

PERSONAL NOTES

SEED YOU WOULD LIKE TO DEVELOP THIS WEEK:

Self-Check

S	M	T	W	T	F	S
☐	☐	☐	☐	☐	☐	☐
☐	☐	☐	☐	☐	☐	☐
☐	☐	☐	☐	☐	☐	☐

PLANTING THE SEED
Plan daily actions that will help you produce the fruit you desire.

WATERING THE SEED
Encouragement from God's Word. Inspiring thoughts. Helpful words from others.

Month of: _____

DAILY APPOINTMENTS AND ACTIVITIES

Sunday..........	Monday..........	Tuesday..........

REMINDERS FOR FAMILY AND HOME

PRAYER GARDEN

REAPING THE HARVEST

Fruit you are seeing in your life this week as a result of God's nurturing and your faithful efforts. *(Be sure to consider little changes.)*

_____
_____
_____
_____
_____
_____
_____

"For we are God's fellow workers; you are God's field."

1 Corinthians 3:9

Wednesday...........	Thursday...........	Friday...........	Saturday...........

PERSONAL NOTES

Seed You Would Like to Develop This Week:

_____

Planting the Seed

Plan daily actions that will help you produce the fruit you desire.

Self-Check

S	M	T	W	T	F	S
☐	☐	☐	☐	☐	☐	☐
☐	☐	☐	☐	☐	☐	☐
☐	☐	☐	☐	☐	☐	☐

Watering the Seed

Encouragement from God's Word. Inspiring thoughts. Helpful words from others.

_____

Month of:

_____

Daily Appointments and Activities

Sunday............

Monday............

Tuesday............

Reminders for Family and Home

Prayer Garden

REAPING
THE
HARVEST

Fruit you are
seeing in your life
this week as a
result of God's
nurturing and your
faithful efforts.
*(Be sure to consider
little changes.)*

_____

_____

_____

_____

_____

_____

*"Give her the reward she has
earned, and let her works bring
praise at the city gate."*

Proverbs 31:31

Wednesday............

_____

_____

_____

_____

_____

_____

_____

_____

_____

_____

_____

Thursday............

_____

_____

_____

_____

_____

_____

_____

_____

_____

_____

_____

Friday............

_____

_____

_____

_____

_____

_____

_____

_____

_____

_____

_____

Saturday............

_____

_____

_____

_____

_____

_____

_____

_____

_____

_____

_____

PERSONAL
NOTES

_____

_____

_____

HIGHLIGHTS FOR THE MONTH OF _____

Sunday	Monday	Tuesday	Wednesday	Thursday	Friday	Saturday

Unscheduled items for this month: _____

BIRTHDAYS & ANNIVERSARIES

Date	Name	Family Traditions	Preparations
_____	_____	_____	_____
_____	_____	_____	_____
_____	_____	_____	_____
_____	_____	_____	_____

HOLIDAYS

_____	_____	_____	_____
_____	_____	_____	_____

Self-Check

S	M	T	W	T	F	S
☐	☐	☐	☐	☐	☐	☐
☐	☐	☐	☐	☐	☐	☐
☐	☐	☐	☐	☐	☐	☐

PLANTING THE SEED

Plan daily actions that will help you produce the fruit you desire.

WATERING THE SEED

Encouragement from God's Word. Inspiring thoughts. Helpful words from others.

Month of:

Sunday...........

Monday...........

Tuesday...........

DAILY APPOINTMENTS AND ACTIVITIES

REMINDERS FOR FAMILY AND HOME

PRAYER GARDEN

REAPING THE HARVEST

Fruit you are seeing in your life this week as a result of God's nurturing and your faithful efforts. *(Be sure to consider little changes.)*

_____
_____
_____
_____
_____
_____
_____

"If you remain in me and my words remain in you, ask whatever you wish, and it will be given you."

John 15:7

Wednesday..........	Thursday..........	Friday..........	Saturday..........

PERSONAL NOTES

_____
_____
_____

SEED YOU WOULD LIKE TO DEVELOP THIS WEEK:

_____

PLANTING THE SEED — Plan daily actions that will help you produce the fruit you desire.

_____

_____

_____

WATERING THE SEED — Encouragement from God's Word. Inspiring thoughts. Helpful words from others.

_____

_____

_____

Month of:

_____

DAILY APPOINTMENTS AND ACTIVITIES

Sunday...........	Monday...........	Tuesday...........

REMINDERS FOR FAMILY AND HOME

PRAYER GARDEN

_____

REAPING THE HARVEST

Fruit you are seeing in your life this week as a result of God's nurturing and your faithful efforts. *(Be sure to consider little changes.)*

_____
_____
_____
_____
_____
_____
_____

"He who works his land will have abundant food, but the one who chases fantasies will have his fill of poverty."

Proverbs 28:19

Wednesday............	Thursday............	Friday............	Saturday............

PERSONAL NOTES

Seed You Would Like to Develop This Week:

Planting the Seed
Plan daily actions that will help you produce the fruit you desire.

Self-Check

S	M	T	W	T	F	S
☐	☐	☐	☐	☐	☐	☐
☐	☐	☐	☐	☐	☐	☐
☐	☐	☐	☐	☐	☐	☐

Watering the Seed
Encouragement from God's Word. Inspiring thoughts. Helpful words from others.

Month of:

Sunday............   Monday............   Tuesday............

Daily Appointments and Activities

Reminders for Family and Home

Prayer Garden

REAPING THE HARVEST

Fruit you are seeing in your life this week as a result of God's nurturing and your faithful efforts.
(Be sure to consider little changes.)

_____
_____
_____
_____
_____
_____
_____

"This is to my Father's glory, that you bear much fruit, showing yourselves to be my disciples."

John 15:8

Wednesday............	Thursday............	Friday............	Saturday............

PERSONAL NOTES

_____
_____
_____

SEED YOU WOULD LIKE TO DEVELOP THIS WEEK:

_____

PLANTING THE SEED

Plan daily actions that will help you produce the fruit you desire.

Self-Check

S	M	T	W	T	F	S
☐	☐	☐	☐	☐	☐	☐
☐	☐	☐	☐	☐	☐	☐
☐	☐	☐	☐	☐	☐	☐

_____
_____
_____

WATERING THE SEED

Encouragement from God's Word. Inspiring thoughts. Helpful words from others.

_____
_____
_____

Month of: _____

Sunday............   Monday............   Tuesday............

DAILY APPOINTMENTS AND ACTIVITIES

REMINDERS FOR FAMILY AND HOME

PRAYER GARDEN

REAPING THE HARVEST

Fruit you are seeing in your life this week as a result of God's nurturing and your faithful efforts.
(Be sure to consider little changes.)

_____
_____
_____
_____
_____
_____
_____

"There is a time for everything, and a season for every activity under heaven."

Ecclesiastes 3:1

Wednesday............

Thursday............

Friday............

Saturday............

PERSONAL NOTES

SEED YOU WOULD LIKE TO DEVELOP THIS WEEK:

_____

S	M	T	W	T	F	S
☐	☐	☐	☐	☐	☐	☐
☐	☐	☐	☐	☐	☐	☐
☐	☐	☐	☐	☐	☐	☐

PLANTING THE SEED

Plan daily actions that will help you produce the fruit you desire.

_____
_____
_____

WATERING THE SEED

Encouragement from God's Word. Inspiring thoughts. Helpful words from others.

_____
_____
_____

Month of: _____

	Sunday............	Monday............	Tuesday............

DAILY APPOINTMENTS AND ACTIVITIES

REMINDERS FOR FAMILY AND HOME

PRAYER GARDEN

REAPING THE HARVEST

Fruit you are seeing in your life this week as a result of God's nurturing and your faithful efforts. *(Be sure to consider little changes.)*

_____
_____
_____
_____
_____
_____

"Then they can train the younger women to love their husbands and children, to be self-controlled and pure, to be busy at home, to be kind, and to be subject to their husbands, so that no one will malign the word of God."

Titus 2:4,5

Wednesday...........	Thursday...........	Friday...........	Saturday...........

PERSONAL NOTES

_____
_____
_____

A corner of this planner reserved for your own space; a place for jotting down a memory, a moment, a highlight that might otherwise be lost.

HIGHLIGHTS FOR THE MONTH OF _____

Sunday	Monday	Tuesday	Wednesday	Thursday	Friday	Saturday

Unscheduled items for this month: _____

BIRTHDAYS & ANNIVERSARIES

Date	Name	Family Traditions	Preparations
_____	_____	_____	_____
_____	_____	_____	_____
_____	_____	_____	_____
_____	_____	_____	_____

HOLIDAYS

| _____ | _____ | _____ | _____ |
| _____ | _____ | _____ | _____ |

SEED YOU WOULD LIKE TO DEVELOP THIS WEEK:

_____

PLANTING THE SEED — Plan daily actions that will help you produce the fruit you desire.

Self-Check

S	M	T	W	T	F	S
☐	☐	☐	☐	☐	☐	☐
☐	☐	☐	☐	☐	☐	☐
☐	☐	☐	☐	☐	☐	☐

WATERING THE SEED — Encouragement from God's Word. Inspiring thoughts. Helpful words from others.

Month of: _____

DAILY APPOINTMENTS AND ACTIVITIES	Sunday..........	Monday..........	Tuesday..........

REMINDERS FOR FAMILY AND HOME

PRAYER GARDEN

REAPING
THE
HARVEST

Fruit you are seeing in your life this week as a result of God's nurturing and your faithful efforts. *(Be sure to consider little changes.)*

_____
_____
_____
_____
_____
_____

"As long as it is day, we must do the work of him who sent me. Night is coming, when no one can work."

John 9:4

Wednesday...........

_____
_____
_____
_____
_____
_____
_____
_____
_____

Thursday...........

_____
_____
_____
_____
_____
_____
_____
_____
_____

Friday...........

_____
_____
_____
_____
_____
_____
_____
_____
_____

Saturday...........

_____
_____
_____
_____
_____
_____
_____
_____
_____

_____
_____
_____

PERSONAL
NOTES

_____
_____
_____

SEED YOU WOULD LIKE TO DEVELOP THIS WEEK:

_____

PLANTING THE SEED

Plan daily actions that will help you produce the fruit you desire.

_____

_____

_____

☐	☐	☐	☐	☐	☐	☐
☐	☐	☐	☐	☐	☐	☐
☐	☐	☐	☐	☐	☐	☐

WATERING THE SEED

Encouragement from God's Word. Inspiring thoughts. Helpful words from others.

_____

_____

_____

Month of:

_____

DAILY APPOINTMENTS AND ACTIVITIES

Sunday..........	Monday...........	Tuesday...........
_____	_____	_____
_____	_____	_____
_____	_____	_____
_____	_____	_____
_____	_____	_____
_____	_____	_____
_____	_____	_____
_____	_____	_____
_____	_____	_____
_____	_____	_____
_____	_____	_____

REMINDERS FOR FAMILY AND HOME

_____	_____	_____
_____	_____	_____
_____	_____	_____

PRAYER GARDEN

_____

_____

_____

REAPING THE HARVEST

Fruit you are seeing in your life this week as a result of God's nurturing and your faithful efforts. *(Be sure to consider little changes.)*

_____

_____

_____

_____

_____

_____

"Make it your ambition to lead a quiet life, to mind your own business and to work with your hands, just as we told you, so that your daily life may win the respect of outsiders..."

1 Thessalonians 4:11,12

Wednesday............

_____
_____
_____
_____
_____
_____
_____
_____
_____
_____

_____
_____
_____

Thursday............

_____
_____
_____
_____
_____
_____
_____
_____
_____
_____

_____
_____
_____

Friday............

_____
_____
_____
_____
_____
_____
_____
_____
_____
_____

_____
_____
_____

Saturday............

_____
_____
_____
_____
_____
_____
_____
_____
_____
_____

_____
_____
_____

PERSONAL NOTES

_____

_____

_____

SEED YOU WOULD LIKE TO DEVELOP THIS WEEK:

_____

Self-Check

S	M	T	W	T	F	S
☐	☐	☐	☐	☐	☐	☐
☐	☐	☐	☐	☐	☐	☐
☐	☐	☐	☐	☐	☐	☐

PLANTING THE SEED — Plan daily actions that will help you produce the fruit you desire.

_____

_____

_____

WATERING THE SEED — Encouragement from God's Word. Inspiring thoughts. Helpful words from others.

_____

_____

_____

Month of: _____

DAILY APPOINTMENTS AND ACTIVITIES

Sunday............	Monday............	Tuesday............

REMINDERS FOR FAMILY AND HOME

PRAYER GARDEN

REAPING THE HARVEST

Fruit you are seeing in your life this week as a result of God's nurturing and your faithful efforts. *(Be sure to consider little changes.)*

_____
_____
_____
_____
_____
_____
_____

"Moreover, when God gives any man wealth and possessions, and enables him to enjoy them, to accept his lot and be happy in his work–this is a gift of God."

Ecclesiastes 5:19

Wednesday...........

_____
_____
_____
_____
_____
_____
_____
_____
_____
_____

_____
_____
_____

Thursday...........

_____
_____
_____
_____
_____
_____
_____
_____
_____
_____

_____
_____
_____

Friday...........

_____
_____
_____
_____
_____
_____
_____
_____
_____
_____

_____
_____
_____

Saturday...........

_____
_____
_____
_____
_____
_____
_____
_____
_____
_____

_____
_____
_____

PERSONAL NOTES

_____
_____
_____

SEED YOU WOULD LIKE TO DEVELOP THIS WEEK:

_____

Self-Check

S	M	T	W	T	F	S
☐	☐	☐	☐	☐	☐	☐
☐	☐	☐	☐	☐	☐	☐
☐	☐	☐	☐	☐	☐	☐

PLANTING THE SEED

Plan daily actions that will help you produce the fruit you desire.

_____

_____

_____

WATERING THE SEED

Encouragement from God's Word. Inspiring thoughts. Helpful words from others.

_____

_____

_____

Month of:

_____

DAILY APPOINTMENTS AND ACTIVITIES

Sunday............	Monday............	Tuesday............
_____	_____	_____
_____	_____	_____
_____	_____	_____
_____	_____	_____
_____	_____	_____
_____	_____	_____
_____	_____	_____
_____	_____	_____
_____	_____	_____
_____	_____	_____
_____	_____	_____
_____	_____	_____

REMINDERS FOR FAMILY AND HOME

_____	_____	_____
_____	_____	_____
_____	_____	_____

PRAYER GARDEN

_____

_____

_____

REAPING THE HARVEST

Fruit you are seeing in your life this week as a result of God's nurturing and your faithful efforts. *(Be sure to consider little changes.)*

_____
_____
_____
_____
_____
_____
_____

"At the present time your plenty will supply what they need, so that in turn their plenty will supply what you need."

2 Corinthians 8:14

Wednesday............

Thursday............

Friday............

Saturday............

PERSONAL NOTES

SEED YOU WOULD LIKE TO DEVELOP THIS WEEK:

_____

PLANTING THE SEED

Plan daily actions that will help you produce the fruit you desire.

Self-Check

S	M	T	W	T	F	S
☐	☐	☐	☐	☐	☐	☐
☐	☐	☐	☐	☐	☐	☐
☐	☐	☐	☐	☐	☐	☐

WATERING THE SEED

Encouragement from God's Word. Inspiring thoughts. Helpful words from others.

Month of: _____

Sunday............   Monday...........   Tuesday...........

DAILY APPOINTMENTS AND ACTIVITIES

REMINDERS FOR FAMILY AND HOME

PRAYER GARDEN

REAPING THE HARVEST

Fruit you are seeing in your life this week as a result of God's nurturing and your faithful efforts. *(Be sure to consider little changes.)*

_____
_____
_____
_____
_____
_____
_____

"God is able to make all grace abound to you, so that in all things at all times, having all that you need, you will abound in every good work."

2 Corinthians 9:8

Wednesday............	Thursday............	Friday............	Saturday............

PERSONAL NOTES

A *corner of this planner reserved for your own space; a place for jotting down a memory, a moment, a highlight that might otherwise be lost.*

HIGHLIGHTS FOR THE MONTH OF _____

Sunday	Monday	Tuesday	Wednesday	Thursday	Friday	Saturday

Unscheduled items for this month: _____

BIRTHDAYS & ANNIVERSARIES

Date	Name	Family Traditions	Preparations
_____	_____	_____	_____
_____	_____	_____	_____
_____	_____	_____	_____
_____	_____	_____	_____

HOLIDAYS

_____	_____	_____	_____
_____	_____	_____	_____

SEED YOU WOULD LIKE TO DEVELOP THIS WEEK:

_____

PLANTING THE SEED

Plan daily actions that will help you produce the fruit you desire.

_____

_____

WATERING THE SEED

Encouragement from God's Word. Inspiring thoughts. Helpful words from others.

_____

_____

_____

Month of: _____

| | Sunday........... | Monday........... | Tuesday........... |

DAILY APPOINTMENTS AND ACTIVITIES

_____

REMINDERS FOR FAMILY AND HOME

PRAYER GARDEN

_____

_____

REAPING
THE
HARVEST

Fruit you are
seeing in your life
this week as a
result of God's
nurturing and your
faithful efforts.
*(Be sure to consider
little changes.)*

_____

_____

_____

_____

_____

_____

*"For the Lord God will bless you
in all your harvest and in all the
work of your hands, and your
joy will be complete."*

Deuteronomy 16:15

Wednesday...........

_____

_____

_____

_____

_____

_____

_____

_____

_____

Thursday...........

_____

_____

_____

_____

_____

_____

_____

_____

_____

Friday...........

_____

_____

_____

_____

_____

_____

_____

_____

_____

Saturday...........

_____

_____

_____

_____

_____

_____

_____

_____

_____

_____

_____

_____

_____

_____

_____

_____

_____

_____

_____

_____

_____

_____

_____

_____

_____

_____

PERSONAL
NOTES

_____

_____

_____

SEED YOU WOULD LIKE TO DEVELOP THIS WEEK:

_____

PLANTING THE SEED

Plan daily actions that will help you produce the fruit you desire.

Self-Check

S	M	T	W	T	F	S
☐	☐	☐	☐	☐	☐	☐
☐	☐	☐	☐	☐	☐	☐
☐	☐	☐	☐	☐	☐	☐

WATERING THE SEED

Encouragement from God's Word. Inspiring thoughts. Helpful words from others.

_____

_____

_____

Month of: _____

DAILY APPOINTMENTS AND ACTIVITIES

Sunday..........	Monday..........	Tuesday..........

REMINDERS FOR FAMILY AND HOME

PRAYER GARDEN

REAPING
THE
HARVEST

Fruit you are seeing in your life this week as a result of God's nurturing and your faithful efforts. *(Be sure to consider little changes.)*

_____
_____
_____
_____
_____
_____
_____

"All over the world this gospel is producing fruit and growing, just as it has been doing among you since the day you heard it."

Colossians 1:6

Wednesday...........

Thursday...........

Friday...........

Saturday...........

PERSONAL
NOTES

SEED YOU WOULD LIKE TO DEVELOP THIS WEEK:

_____

PLANTING THE SEED

Plan daily actions that will help you produce the fruit you desire.

Self-Check

S	M	T	W	T	F	S
☐	☐	☐	☐	☐	☐	☐
☐	☐	☐	☐	☐	☐	☐
☐	☐	☐	☐	☐	☐	☐

WATERING THE SEED

Encouragement from God's Word. Inspiring thoughts. Helpful words from others.

_____
_____
_____

Month of: _____

DAILY APPOINTMENTS AND ACTIVITIES

Sunday............

Monday............

Tuesday............

REMINDERS FOR FAMILY AND HOME

PRAYER GARDEN

REAPING THE HARVEST

Fruit you are seeing in your life this week as a result of God's nurturing and your faithful efforts.
(Be sure to consider little changes.)

_____
_____
_____
_____
_____
_____
_____

"But whoso looketh into the perfect law of liberty and continueth therein, he being not a forgetful hearer, but a doer of the work, this man shall be blessed in his deed."

James 1:25

Wednesday............

Thursday............

Friday............

Saturday............

PERSONAL NOTES

SEED YOU WOULD LIKE TO DEVELOP THIS WEEK:

_____

Self-Check

S	M	T	W	T	F	S
☐	☐	☐	☐	☐	☐	☐
☐	☐	☐	☐	☐	☐	☐
☐	☐	☐	☐	☐	☐	☐

PLANTING THE SEED
Plan daily actions that will help you produce the fruit you desire.

_____
_____
_____

WATERING THE SEED
Encouragement from God's Word. Inspiring thoughts. Helpful words from others.

_____
_____
_____

Month of:

_____

DAILY APPOINTMENTS AND ACTIVITIES

Sunday...........	Monday...........	Tuesday...........
_____	_____	_____
_____	_____	_____
_____	_____	_____
_____	_____	_____
_____	_____	_____
_____	_____	_____
_____	_____	_____
_____	_____	_____
_____	_____	_____
_____	_____	_____
_____	_____	_____

REMINDERS FOR FAMILY AND HOME

_____	_____	_____
_____	_____	_____

PRAYER GARDEN

_____
_____
_____

REAPING
THE
HARVEST

Fruit you are
seeing in your life
this week as a
result of God's
nurturing and your
faithful efforts.
*(Be sure to consider
little changes.)*

_____

_____

_____

_____

_____

_____

_____

*"For we are God's fellow workers;
you are God's field."*

1 Corinthians 3:9

Wednesday............

_____

_____

_____

_____

_____

_____

_____

_____

_____

_____

_____

_____

_____

Thursday............

_____

_____

_____

_____

_____

_____

_____

_____

_____

_____

_____

_____

_____

Friday............

_____

_____

_____

_____

_____

_____

_____

_____

_____

_____

_____

_____

_____

Saturday............

_____

_____

_____

_____

_____

_____

_____

_____

_____

_____

_____

_____

_____

PERSONAL
NOTES

_____

_____

_____

SEED YOU WOULD LIKE TO DEVELOP THIS WEEK:

_____

Self-Check

S	M	T	W	T	F	S
☐	☐	☐	☐	☐	☐	☐
☐	☐	☐	☐	☐	☐	☐
☐	☐	☐	☐	☐	☐	☐

PLANTING THE SEED

Plan daily actions that will help you produce the fruit you desire.

_____

_____

_____

WATERING THE SEED

Encouragement from God's Word. Inspiring thoughts. Helpful words from others.

_____

_____

_____

Month of:

_____

DAILY APPOINTMENTS AND ACTIVITIES

Sunday..........	Monday..........	Tuesday..........
_____	_____	_____
_____	_____	_____
_____	_____	_____
_____	_____	_____
_____	_____	_____
_____	_____	_____
_____	_____	_____
_____	_____	_____
_____	_____	_____
_____	_____	_____
_____	_____	_____

REMINDERS FOR FAMILY AND HOME

_____	_____	_____
_____	_____	_____
_____	_____	_____

PRAYER GARDEN

_____

_____

_____

REAPING THE HARVEST

Fruit you are seeing in your life this week as a result of God's nurturing and your faithful efforts. *(Be sure to consider little changes.)*

_____
_____
_____
_____
_____
_____
_____

"He [the gardener] cuts off every branch in me that bears no fruit, while every branch that does bear fruit he trims clean so that it will be even more fruitful."

John 15:2

Wednesday............ | Thursday............ | Friday............ | Saturday............

PERSONAL NOTES

Books, Tapes, & Videos

I am interested in:
At times a friend, pastor, radio speaker, or Bible study leader recommends a book or material that interests you. Writing it down here will help you pursue it at a later time.

Title	Author	Publisher	Where Available

Crafts, Sewing, & Decorating Ideas

Occasionally you may see a craft, sewing, or decorating idea that sparks your interest. Jotting down the essence will give you a springboard for your own creativity when the time is right for working on such a project.

Gift Ideas

Good gift ideas often come when you're not looking for them. Writing them down throughout the year will make shopping easier for that special someone.

Name	Gift Idea	Where Available

Gracious Hospitality

When we extend our heart through our home, we want our guests to feel warmly welcome, comfortable, and special. A ready reference of unique ideas, from simple to elaborate, will help you meet the need of these special occasions.

Here are some ideas to get you started: Table decorations; individual place cards that reflect the personality of your guests; menu ideas for outdoor barbeques; candlelight dinner for two; family dinners for twenty-two; children's birthday party themes; welcome baskets for overnight guests filled with necessities and fun things of particular interest to your guests.

Menu Ideas

For the "what sounds good" syndrome: writing down recipes you would like to try, as well as favorite family dishes, can make menu planning faster and easier. These pages are a key to quickly unlock the cookbook and page number of a desired recipe so that you won't have to search each time you need it.

MAIN DISH   Cookbook & Page

VEGETABLES   Cookbook & Page

BREADS   Cookbook & Page

SALADS & FRUIT	Cookbook & Page	DESSERTS	Cookbook & Page

Special Telephone Numbers for Quick Reference

Fire

Ambulance

Police

Highway Patrol

Poison Control

Time

Weather

Family Doctors and Dentists

Repairmen

Kids' Schools

Relatives' numbers

A *corner of this planner reserved for your own space; a place for jotting down a memory, a moment, a highlight that might otherwise be lost.*

1994

JANUARY

S	M	T	W	T	F	S
						1
2	3	4	5	6	7	8
9	10	11	12	13	14	15
16	17	18	19	20	21	22
23/30	24/31	25	26	27	28	29

FEBRUARY

S	M	T	W	T	F	S
		1	2	3	4	5
6	7	8	9	10	11	12
13	14	15	16	17	18	19
20	21	22	23	24	25	26
27	28					

MARCH

S	M	T	W	T	F	S
		1	2	3	4	5
6	7	8	9	10	11	12
13	14	15	16	17	18	19
20	21	22	23	24	25	26
27	28	29	30	31		

APRIL

S	M	T	W	T	F	S
					1	2
3	4	5	6	7	8	9
10	11	12	13	14	15	16
17	18	19	20	21	22	23
24	25	26	27	28	29	30

MAY

S	M	T	W	T	F	S
1	2	3	4	5	6	7
8	9	10	11	12	13	14
15	16	17	18	19	20	21
22	23	24	25	26	27	28
29	30	31				

JUNE

S	M	T	W	T	F	S
			1	2	3	4
5	6	7	8	9	10	11
12	13	14	15	16	17	18
19	20	21	22	23	24	25
26	27	28	29	30		

JULY

S	M	T	W	T	F	S
					1	2
3	4	5	6	7	8	9
10	11	12	13	14	15	16
17	18	19	20	21	22	23
24/31	25	26	27	28	29	30

AUGUST

S	M	T	W	T	F	S
	1	2	3	4	5	6
7	8	9	10	11	12	13
14	15	16	17	18	19	20
21	22	23	24	25	26	27
28	29	30	31			

SEPTEMBER

S	M	T	W	T	F	S
				1	2	3
4	5	6	7	8	9	10
11	12	13	14	15	16	17
18	19	20	21	22	23	24
25	26	27	28	29	30	

OCTOBER

S	M	T	W	T	F	S
						1
2	3	4	5	6	7	8
9	10	11	12	13	14	15
16	17	18	19	20	21	22
23	24	25	26	27	28	29
30	31					

NOVEMBER

S	M	T	W	T	F	S
		1	2	3	4	5
6	7	8	9	10	11	12
13	14	15	16	17	18	19
20	21	22	23	24	25	26
27	28	29	30			

DECEMBER

S	M	T	W	T	F	S
				1	2	3
4	5	6	7	8	9	10
11	12	13	14	15	16	17
18	19	20	21	22	23	24
25	26	27	28	29	30	31

1995

JANUARY

S	M	T	W	T	F	S
1	2	3	4	5	6	7
8	9	10	11	12	13	14
15	16	17	18	19	20	21
22	23	24	25	26	27	28
29	30	31				

FEBRUARY

S	M	T	W	T	F	S
			1	2	3	4
5	6	7	8	9	10	11
12	13	14	15	16	17	18
19	20	21	22	23	24	25
26	27	28				

MARCH

S	M	T	W	T	F	S
			1	2	3	4
5	6	7	8	9	10	11
12	13	14	15	16	17	18
19	20	21	22	23	24	25
26	27	28	29	30	31	

APRIL

S	M	T	W	T	F	S
						1
2	3	4	5	6	7	8
9	10	11	12	13	14	15
16	17	18	19	20	21	22
23/30	24	25	26	27	28	29

MAY

S	M	T	W	T	F	S
	1	2	3	4	5	6
7	8	9	10	11	12	13
14	15	16	17	18	19	20
21	22	23	24	25	26	27
28	29	30	31			

JUNE

S	M	T	W	T	F	S
				1	2	3
4	5	6	7	8	9	10
11	12	13	14	15	16	17
18	19	20	21	22	23	24
25	26	27	28	29	30	

JULY

S	M	T	W	T	F	S
						1
2	3	4	5	6	7	8
9	10	11	12	13	14	15
16	17	18	19	20	21	22
23/30	24/31	25	26	27	28	29

AUGUST

S	M	T	W	T	F	S
		1	2	3	4	5
6	7	8	9	10	11	12
13	14	15	16	17	18	19
20	21	22	23	24	25	26
27	28	29	30	31		

SEPTEMBER

S	M	T	W	T	F	S
					1	2
3	4	5	6	7	8	9
10	11	12	13	14	15	16
17	18	19	20	21	22	23
24	25	26	27	28	29	30

OCTOBER

S	M	T	W	T	F	S
1	2	3	4	5	6	7
8	9	10	11	12	13	14
15	16	17	18	19	20	21
22	23	24	25	26	27	28
29	30	31				

NOVEMBER

S	M	T	W	T	F	S
			1	2	3	4
5	6	7	8	9	10	11
12	13	14	15	16	17	18
19	20	21	22	23	24	25
26	27	28	29	30		

DECEMBER

S	M	T	W	T	F	S
					1	2
3	4	5	6	7	8	9
10	11	12	13	14	15	16
17	18	19	20	21	22	23
24/31	25	26	27	28	29	30

1996

JANUARY

S	M	T	W	T	F	S
	1	2	3	4	5	6
7	8	9	10	11	12	13
14	15	16	17	18	19	20
21	22	23	24	25	26	27
28	29	30	31			

FEBRUARY

S	M	T	W	T	F	S
				1	2	3
4	5	6	7	8	9	10
11	12	13	14	15	16	17
18	19	20	21	22	23	24
25	26	27	28	29		

MARCH

S	M	T	W	T	F	S
					1	2
3	4	5	6	7	8	9
10	11	12	13	14	15	16
17	18	19	20	21	22	23
24/31	25	26	27	28	29	30

APRIL

S	M	T	W	T	F	S
	1	2	3	4	5	6
7	8	9	10	11	12	13
14	15	16	17	18	19	20
21	22	23	24	25	26	27
28	29	30				

MAY

S	M	T	W	T	F	S
			1	2	3	4
5	6	7	8	9	10	11
12	13	14	15	16	17	18
19	20	21	22	23	24	25
26	27	28	29	30	31	

JUNE

S	M	T	W	T	F	S
						1
2	3	4	5	6	7	8
9	10	11	12	13	14	15
16	17	18	19	20	21	22
23/30	24	25	26	27	28	29

JULY

S	M	T	W	T	F	S
	1	2	3	4	5	6
7	8	9	10	11	12	13
14	15	16	17	18	19	20
21	22	23	24	25	26	27
28	29	30	31			

AUGUST

S	M	T	W	T	F	S
				1	2	3
4	5	6	7	8	9	10
11	12	13	14	15	16	17
18	19	20	21	22	23	24
25	26	27	28	29	30	31

SEPTEMBER

S	M	T	W	T	F	S
1	2	3	4	5	6	7
8	9	10	11	12	13	14
15	16	17	18	19	20	21
22	23	24	25	26	27	28
29	30					

OCTOBER

S	M	T	W	T	F	S
		1	2	3	4	5
6	7	8	9	10	11	12
13	14	15	16	17	18	19
20	21	22	23	24	25	26
27	28	29	30	31		

NOVEMBER

S	M	T	W	T	F	S
					1	2
3	4	5	6	7	8	9
10	11	12	13	14	15	16
17	18	19	20	21	22	23
24	25	26	27	28	29	30

DECEMBER

S	M	T	W	T	F	S
1	2	3	4	5	6	7
8	9	10	11	12	13	14
15	16	17	18	19	20	21
22	23	24	25	26	27	28
29	30	31				

Save on Your Next Package of Seeds

Clip these coupons and use them toward your next two purchases of Focus on the Family's calendar planner, *The Fruit of Her Hands.* The first coupon is for you; the second is for a friend. After all, there's nothing sweeter than harvesting the fruit of excellent organization.

Coupons may be redeemed only at Christian bookstores.

FOR A
FRIEND

The FRUIT OF HER HANDS

$1.00 OFF   **$1.00 OFF**

This coupon is good for ONE DOLLAR off
THE FRUIT OF HER HANDS.
Present this coupon when you make the
purchase at your local Christian bookstore.
Expires January 31, 1995.

Note to Retailer: To receive credit to your account for redeemed coupons, please attach coupons to a summary sheet listing your store name, account number, address and telephone number. Send to your WORD PUBLISHING representative or WORD PUBLISHING, P.O. Box 2518, Waco, TX 76702-2518, Attention: Jo Nell Hale. **Coupons must be returned to Word Inc. by February 28, 1995.**

_____   _____
Store clerk initials   Date

FOR WHEN
YOU REORDER

$1.00 OFF   **$1.00 OFF**

This coupon is good for ONE DOLLAR off
THE FRUIT OF HER HANDS.
Present this coupon when you make the
purchase at your local Christian bookstore.
Expires January 31, 1995.

Note to Retailer: To receive credit to your account for redeemed coupons, please attach coupons to a summary sheet listing your store name, account number, address and telephone number. Send to your WORD PUBLISHING representative or WORD PUBLISHING, P.O. Box 2518, Waco, TX 76702-2518, Attention: Jo Nell Hale. **Coupons must be returned to Word Inc. by February 28, 1995.**

_____   _____
Store clerk initials   Date